A Skyscraper Reaches Up

Kylie Burns

Crabtree Publishing Company

www.crabtreebooks.com

Be An Engineer!
Designing to Solve Problems

Author: Kylie Burns

Series research and development:
Janine Deschenes and Reagan Miller

Editorial director: Kathy Middleton

Editors: Petrice Custance, Crystal Sikkens

Proofreader: Janine Deschenes

Design: Katherine Berti

Photo research: Crystal Sikkens

Production coordinator and prepress technician:
Tammy McGarr

Print coordinator: Margaret Amy Salter

Photographs:

AP Images: Naoki Maeda p15

iStock: © DragonImages p6; © franckreporter p22 (bottom)

Library of Congress: Chicago Architectural Photographing
Company p17

Shutterstock: © elbud p5

Wikimedia Commons: AngMoKio p7 (bkgd); Sergio~commonswiki
p12; Ben Grey p13

All other images by Shutterstock

Animation and digital resources produced for
Crabtree Publishing by Plug-In Media

Library and Archives Canada Cataloguing in Publication

Burns, Kylie, author
    A skyscraper reaches up / Kylie Burns.

(Be an engineer! designing to solve problems)
Issued in print and electronic formats.
Includes index.
ISBN 978-0-7787-2904-4 (hardcover).--
ISBN 978-0-7787-2939-6 (softcover).--
ISBN 978-1-4271-1852-3 (HTML)

    1. Skyscrapers--Juvenile literature. 2. Skyscrapers--Design
and construction--Juvenile literature. I. Title.

TH1615.B87 2017   j690   C2016-907065-4
                                        C2016-907066-2

Library of Congress Cataloging-in-Publication Data

Names: Burns, Kylie, author.
Title: A skyscraper reaches up / Kylie Burns.
Description: New York, New York : Crabtree Publishing Company, [2017] |
    Series: Be an engineer! designing to solve problems | Audience: Ages 7-10.
    | Audience: Grades 4 to 6. | Includes index.
Identifiers: LCCN 2016055766 (print) | LCCN 2016056168 (ebook) |
    ISBN 9780778729044 (reinforced library binding : alk. paper) |
    ISBN 9780778729396 (pbk. : alk. paper) |
    ISBN 9781427118523 (Electronic HTML)
Subjects: LCSH: Skyscrapers--Design and construction--Juvenile literature. |
    Skyscrapers--Juvenile literature.
Classification: LCC TH1615 .B87 2017 (print) | LCC TH1615 (ebook) | DDC
    720/.483--dc23
LC record available at https://lccn.loc.gov/2016055766

Crabtree Publishing Company

www.crabtreebooks.com   1-800-387-7650

Printed in Canada/032017/BF20170111

Published in Canada
Crabtree Publishing
616 Welland Ave.
St. Catharines, Ontario
L2M 5V6

Published in the United States
Crabtree Publishing
PMB 59051
350 Fifth Avenue, 59th Floor
New York, New York 10118

Published in the United Kingdom
Crabtree Publishing
Maritime House
Basin Road North, Hove
BN41 1WR

Published in Australia
Crabtree Publishing
3 Charles Street
Coburg North
VIC 3058

Contents

Hi, I'm Ava and this is Finn. Get ready for an inside look at the world of engineering! The Be an Engineer! series explores how engineers build structures to solve problems.

After reading this book, join us online at Crabtree Plus to help us solve real-world engineering challenges! Just use the Digital Code on page 23 in this book.

Nowhere But Up

Jordan is sad to learn that the park near his house will be closing soon. The land the park is on will be used to build new office spaces and stores. Now Jordan will have to travel much farther to go to a different park. Jordan wishes he didn't have to lose his favorite place to play.

Jordan starts to think of ways that would save the park, but still provide space for new offices and stores.

Problem Solved!

Jordan wonders why the new offices and stores can't be located in some of the empty buildings in his town, or maybe they could be built underground. Then he thinks about a skyscraper. A skyscraper is a very tall building with about 50 or more stories, or floors, stacked on top of each other. Instead of using up new ground, skyscrapers stretch up and create rooms in the sky!

Did you know?

Sailors used to call the tallest **sail** on a ship the "skyscraper." That's where our tallest buildings get their name!

What Is an Engineer?

Some people, like Jordan, enjoy solving problems. People who do this for a living are called engineers. An engineer solves problems and meets people's needs using math, science, and creative thinking. When a problem needs to be solved, an engineer designs things that get the job done.

All Kinds of Engineers

There are many different kinds of engineers, including some who create roads, spaceships, bridges, and even medicine. Not all engineers are the same. Some engineers design the materials for buildings and structures such as skyscrapers. Others design their shape and size. Most engineers work as part of a team.

Engineers designed Taiwan's tallest skyscraper, Taipei 101, in the shape of a giant bamboo stalk!

Steps to Solving Problems

Problems aren't always easy to solve. All engineers follow the same set of steps to solve a problem. The set of steps is called the Engineering Design Process. The steps in this process can be repeated over and over until the solution is both safe and **effective**. Making mistakes is often part of this process.

The Engineering Design Process

1 ASK
Ask questions and gather information about the problem you are trying to solve.

2 BRAINSTORM
Work with a group to come up with different ideas to solve the problem. Choose the best solution.

3 PLAN AND MAKE A MODEL
Create a plan to carry out your solution. Draw a diagram and gather materials. Make a **model** of your solution.

4 TEST AND IMPROVE
Test your model and record the results. Using the results, improve, or make your design better. Retest your improved design.

5 COMMUNICATE
Share your design with others.

Asking Questions

Engineers ask questions and gather information so they can make the best choices when solving a problem. When engineers want to create more living or work space in a crowded city, they need to find out what the **environment** in the area is like. For example, engineers need to know whether **earthquakes** or severe weather is common.

Asking questions and gathering information is the first step in the Engineering Design Process.

Brainstorming

Once engineers have gathered their information, they brainstorm, or discuss possible solutions to the problem with others.

A diagram, such as this one, is useful for engineers to keep track of ideas while they are brainstorming.

Problem
There is not enough living and working space in a crowded city

Make the city larger to include more land for new buildings

Build a skyscraper

Create buildings underground

Fix up old buildings and make them into new homes or offices

Planning

If the brainstorming team decided a skyscraper was the best solution, engineers must then begin planning to build it. They will need to determine the height of the skyscraper, and whether it will need extra supports to keep it **stable** during earthquakes or high winds. Supports may include **braces** or a deep, strong **foundation**.

Did you know?

Skyscrapers today are often built using steel and concrete. Concrete is a hard building material made from loose stones, cement, and water.

Supports known as x-braces can be seen on the outside of this building.

Different Shapes

Early skyscrapers were often rectangular or pyramid shaped. The bottoms of the buildings were designed to support the weight of the whole building. Today, engineers design skyscrapers with tube-shaped columns that are placed inside the middle of the building. This allows the weight of the building to be supported by the whole structure. With this type of design, skyscrapers can be built higher than ever before.

(left) The Willis Tower in Chicago, Illinois, is a skyscraper with tube-shaped columns in its center. It has 110 floors and 104 elevators.

Creating a Model

Before any construction begins, engineers create a model of the skyscraper. A model is a **representation** of a real object. Engineers may design a model with computer software or build a small **3-D** model of the skyscraper. A model allows engineers to test their design and make improvements.

An engineer can also use a model to explain the design to others.

Testing and Improving

Engineers test their model against the **forces** that may affect a skyscraper, such as wind. By recreating these forces, engineers can find out if the skyscraper will be strong enough to stand up against them. Sometimes engineers test their model on a shake table, which acts like an earthquake by shaking the model.

If the model is strong and stable, it will remain standing on the moving shake table.

Sharing the Results

The last step in the Engineering Design Process is to communicate, or share your results. This helps engineers determine which designs work and which don't. Over time, sharing results has helped improve the designs of skyscrapers, making them taller and more stable.

By sharing information, engineers all over the world have been able to create taller and taller skyscrapers, like the Burj Khalifa in Dubai.

Did you know?

The Burj Khalifa is the tallest skyscraper in the world at 2,717 feet (829.8 meters). It takes workers three months just to clean the windows!

Past to Present

Early skyscrapers were made of heavy materials such as stone, wood, and iron. They were not very tall because the walls and floors could not support the weight of many stories. When stronger and lighter steel was introduced, engineers discovered they could build higher and higher into the sky.

In 1871, most of the wooden buildings in Chicago burnt down during a huge fire. After, William Le Baron Jenney designed the first skyscraper built with a steel **frame**.

Step by Step

It is extremely important that engineers closely follow each step in the Engineering Design Process. If they don't, important information may be missed and dangerous mistakes can be made. If a mistake is made in the design of a skyscraper, it could lead to disaster.

The Engineering Design Process

1 ASK
Ask questions and gather information about the problem you are trying to solve.

2 BRAINSTORM
Work with a group to come up with different ideas to solve the problem. Choose the best solution.

3 PLAN AND MAKE A MODEL
Create a plan to carry out your solution. Draw a diagram and gather materials. Make a **model** of your solution.

4 TEST AND IMPROVE
Test your model and record the results. Using the results, improve, or make your design better. Retest your improved design.

5 COMMUNICATE
Share your design with others.

Close Call

The Citicorp Center skyscraper in New York City was built in 1977. Not long after it was built, an engineering student studied the building's design and realized that if a strong wind struck the corners of the building in a certain way, it was in danger of collapsing. The engineers discovered the student was right, and emergency repairs were made to strengthen the building.

The white Citicorp Center building still stands today among New York's many skyscrapers.

Model Activity

The example of the Citicorp Center skyscraper shows how important it is that engineers test their model for every possible force that may affect the skyscraper once it is built. Try building your own model of a skyscraper and test its strength.

You will need:

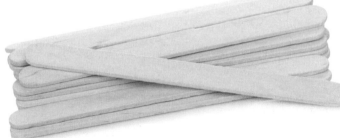

popsicle sticks

wood glue

book

Instructions

1. Arrange four popsicle sticks in a square. Overlap the corners so that each edge sticks out the width of a popsicle stick.

2. Glue the sticks together at each corner. Allow to dry. Place a stick diagonally across the square and glue at both ends. This is a brace. Continue making squares.

3. Arrange four squares like a cube, so they are standing to form the four walls of one level. Glue the squares together. Make at least five more cubes.

4. Carefully place one cube on top of another and glue in place. Allow to dry before adding the next cube.

- Add weight, such as a book, to the top of your skyscraper. What happens?
- How could you strengthen your skyscraper if the weight of the book made it collapse?

Avoiding Disaster

By sharing ideas and working as a team, engineers were able to avoid disaster at the Citicorp Center building. Today, engineers are able to check on skyscrapers using satellites in space. Satellites can track the slightest change in how a building is standing.

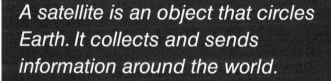

A satellite is an object that circles Earth. It collects and sends information around the world.

Learning More

Books

Hurley, Michael. *The World's Most Amazing Skyscrapers*. Raintree, 2012.

Johmann, Carol, A. *Skyscrapers! Super Structures to Design & Build.* Williamson Publishing Co., 2001.

Oxlade, Chris. *Skyscrapers, Uncovering Technology*. Firefly Books, 2004.

Websites

Learn how skyscrapers defy earthquakes and more: **http://discoverykids.com/articles/how-high-are-skyscrapers-built/**

This site has interesting facts about some of the world's most amazing skyscrapers and how they are built: **www.pbs.org/wgbh/buildingbig/skyscraper/**

For fun engineering challenges, activities, and more, enter the code at the Crabtree Plus website below.

www.crabtreeplus.com/be-an-engineer

Your code is:
bae04

Glossary

Note: Some boldfaced words are defined where they appear in the book.

3-D (THREE-DEE) *adjective* Short for three-dimensional, an object that has length, width, and height

brace (breys) *noun* Something that supports or holds something in place

earthquake (URTH-kweyk) *noun* A series of vibrations that begin in Earth's crust

effective (ih-FEK-tiv) *adjective* Producing the correct result

environment (en-VAHY-ern-muh-nt) *noun* The natural surroundings of things

force (fohrs) *noun* The amount of push or pull acting on an object

foundation (foun-DEY-shuh-n) *noun* The ground or base a thing is built on

frame (freym) *noun* The supporting parts of a building

model (MOD-l) *noun* A representation of a real object

representation (rep-ri-zen-TEY-shuh-n) *noun* Something that stands in place for something else

sail (seyl) *noun* Fabric on a ship that catches wind to move the ship

stable (STEY-buh-l) *adjective* Does not change position

A noun is a person, place, or thing. An adjective is a word that tells you what something is like.

Index